A User's Guide to the Book of Common Prayer

The Holy Eucharist Rites I and II

Christopher L. Webber

MOREHOUSE PUBLISHING

Morehouse Publishing
P.O. Box 1321
Harrisburg, PA 17105

ISBN 0-8192-1695-X

Printed in the United States of America

06 07 08   7 6 5 4

Contents

NOTE: Because the text of Rite I is longer than the text of Rite II (even though the Penitential Order is included only with Rite II) and equal space has been given to both, there is more space available for commentary on Rite II. The commentary on Rite II, however, is often equally relevant to Rite I (and vice versa) so users of one Rite can often benefit by looking at the commentary on the other as well.

Introduction to the Eucharist

The Holy Eucharist has its roots in two ancient Jewish patterns of worship: the synagogue service and the seder meal. The first part of the eucharist is based on one and the second part on the other.

The first part of the eucharist, subtitled "The Word of God," centers on the reading and proclamation of God's word. The Jews in exile in Babylon in the sixth century before Christ kept alive their sense of identity by reading the words of the prophets and the stories of their origins and history. Gradually the custom developed of reading prayers, psalms, and scripture in a regular pattern and from this the first synagogue service emerged. By the time of Jesus, the synagogue had a central place in every Jewish community.

It was expected that every adult male would be able to read the scriptures and to comment on them. Most American Christians are familiar with the way in which Jewish boys and girls today prepare for a bar mitzvah or bas mitzvah ceremony in which they become sons or daughters of the commandment, those who are able to read and teach God's word. We remember that Jesus was asked to fulfill that responsibility when he returned home to the synagogue in Nazareth (Luke 4:16-20). Since many of the first Christians were Jews, it was very natural for them to continue to read the Hebrew scriptures and, at an early date, to begin to read their own writings as well.

Following this same pattern, in the Holy Eucharist, after opening prayers and hymns of praise, we are given two or three lessons interspersed with psalms or hymns or anthems which provide opportunity to reflect on what has been heard and to respond.

The sermon then provides opportunity to proclaim God's word in terms related to our lives today and the Creed enables the whole congregation to respond to what they have heard with a statement of faith.

The pattern for the first part of the service is as follows:

> Opening hymn
> Salutation
> Gloria, Kyrie, or Trisagion
> Prayer (Collect for the Day)
> Reading (Old Testament)
> Psalm, hymn, or anthem
> Reading (Epistle)
> Psalm, hymn, or anthem
> Reading (Gospel)
> Sermon
> Creed

The second part of the eucharist, subtitled "The Holy Communion," follows a different pattern. Scholars differ as to whether the Last Supper was a seder meal commemorating the Passover and deliverance from Egypt, but it is clear that the events of the Passover were very central to the meaning of what Jesus and the disciples did on their last evening together. If it was a full Passover celebration, the meal would have included roast lamb and bitter herbs and other symbolic food. But all formal Jewish meals included a giving thanks for the bread and cup, a breaking of the bread, and a sharing of the cup. The least we can say about the Last Supper is that it was a Jewish meal closely connected to the Passover celebration. The blessing and breaking of bread and the blessing and sharing of a cup of wine would have been observed as usual, but this meal must have been deeply influenced by the celebration of the Passover. Looking back, the disciples would have come to understand the deep relationship between the Passover celebration of those great acts through which God's people were set free from slavery, and the crucifixion and resurrection of Jesus through which God has set us free from sin and death. Whenever the first Christians met to share a meal, they would have broken bread in the familiar way, and remembered those great events, and recognized with joy Christ's presence in their midst.

The pattern the first Christians followed is a very simple one which occurs over and over in the gospels and epistles: "He took bread, and when he had given thanks, he broke it, and gave it to his disciples. He took the cup, gave thanks, and gave it to them."* Four actions are described: taking, blessing, breaking, and giving. The second part of the eucharist is just those four actions. It is an activity in which we take part, not a performance that we watch.

The pattern is as follows:

He took bread (the cup)	The Offertory
and when he had given thanks	The Great Thanksgiving
he broke it	The Breaking of the Bread
and gave it to them	Communion

The words that accompany one of these four actions may require the better part of four pages, as the eucharistic prayers do, or a mere two lines, as does the breaking of the bread, but it is the action that matters. The words simply give expression to the action and provide means for the congregation to understand and respond.

The celebration of the eucharist is built around a fundamentally uncomplicated structure: there are two segments, one alternating readings and response, the other consisting of four simple actions. The ceremonies that embellish this pattern may be as elaborate as human art can imagine, but however elaborate they may be, they are intended to clarify the meaning and add dramatic impact. The eucharist can also be celebrated without vestments, music, or ceremony at the bedside of a hospital patient or, as the first Jamestown settlers did, on a plank nailed between two trees. Every celebration of the eucharist is a compromise between the glorious art that has been developed for it and the time and resources available to a particular congregation, but the simple basic structure of the service remains the same and should always be kept in mind.

---

*Feeding the five thousand and the four thousand (Matthew 14:9, 15:36, Mark 6:41, 8:6, Luke 9:16, John 6:11); the Last Supper (Matthew 26:26-29, Mark 14:22-25, Luke 22:19-20); the road to Emmaus (Luke 24-30) and I Corinthians 11:23-25.

Rite I and Rite II

Language: The most obvious difference between Rite I and Rite II is the language. Rite I uses the language of sixteenth- and seventeenth-century England: the language of Shakespeare, the King James Version of the Bible, and the first English Prayer Book. This language is part of the heritage of the English-speaking world and still adds a sense of mystery and "special-ness" that can enhance and deepen the experience of worship. Rite II uses more contemporary language. Some will prefer the greater clarity of Rite II while others will prefer the sense of mystery conveyed by Rite I. Both are aspects of our relationship with God but no human language can adequately express both the closeness to us of the God who enters the world and the infinite mystery of the God who created it.

Form: While the outline or structure of the two Rites is the same, the prayers of Rite I provide less opportunity for congregational participation and there are fewer alternatives.

Theology: The emphasis of the first English Prayer Books was much more heavily on human sin and God's judgment. Rite II attempts to restore the emphasis of the early church on human thankfulness for God's love and forgiveness. Here again, both emphases are aspects of our relationship with God; the difficulty for human beings is to hold both these aspects in balance or to include both in any one service.

The Holy Eucharist: Rite One

The Word of God

A hymn, psalm, or anthem may be sung.

The people standing, the Celebrant may say

           Blessed be God: Father, Son, and Holy Spirit.
People   And blessed be his kingdom, now and for ever.
           Amen.

In place of the above, from Easter Day through the Day of Pentecost

Celebrant Alleluia. Christ is risen.
People   The Lord is risen indeed. Alleluia.

In Lent and on other penitential occasions

Celebrant Bless the Lord who forgiveth all our sins.
People   His mercy endureth for ever.

The Celebrant says

Almighty God, unto whom all hearts are open, all desires
known, and from whom no secrets are hid: Cleanse the
thoughts of our hearts by the inspiration of thy Holy Spirit,
that we may perfectly love thee, and worthily magnify thy
holy Name; through Christ our Lord. *Amen.*

The Word of God

The first half of the eucharist centers on the Word of God, read to us from the Bible and proclaimed to us from the pulpit.

Entrance and Salutation
Most events begin as people gather and greet each other. Clergy, choir, and acolytes may enter in a formal procession with a hymn or other music to mark the beginning of the service in a dramatic way. When all are in place, a formal greeting is exchanged. The words of this greeting change during Easter and penitential seasons such as Lent. The service can also begin with the Litany or the Penitential Order (cf. commentary on pages 15-16)

Collect for Purity
Rite I opens with an ancient prayer that was part of the priest's preparation in the Latin mass used in England before the Reformation. Archbishop Thomas Cranmer made it the first public prayer of the service, and it has remained a distinctive part of Anglican worship ever since. It serves here, too, as an act of preparation, reminding us that all our thoughts and desires are known to God before we begin to pray and that it is only by the cleansing power of the Spirit that our prayers and praises can be perfected and made worthy. Even in this brief prayer the Trinitarian nature of Christian worship is clearly stated: our lives lie open before God our Creator, the Holy Spirit acts to purify them, and it is through Jesus Christ that all our worship is offered.

Then the Ten Commandments (page 317) may be said, or the following

Hear what our Lord Jesus Christ saith:
Thou shalt love the Lord thy God with all thy heart, and with all thy soul, and with all thy mind. This is the first and great commandment. And the second is like unto it: Thou shalt love thy neighbor as thyself. On these two commandments hang all the Law and the Prophets.

Here is sung or said

Lord, have mercy upon us.		Kyrie eleison.
Christ, have mercy upon us.	*or*	*Christe eleison.*
Lord, have mercy upon us.		Kyrie eleison.

or this

Holy God,
Holy and Mighty,
Holy Immortal One,
Have mercy upon us.

When appointed, the following hymn or some other song of praise is sung or said, in addition to, or in place of, the preceding, all standing

Glory be to God on high,
  and on earth peace, good will towards men.

We praise thee, we bless thee,
  we worship thee,
  we glorify thee,
  we give thanks to thee for thy great glory,
O Lord God, heavenly King, God the Father Almighty.

O Lord, the only-begotten Son, Jesus Christ;
O Lord God, Lamb of God, Son of the Father,
  that takest away the sins of the world,
  have mercy upon us.

Summary of the Law

The first revision of the English Prayer Book, in 1552, added the Ten Commandments to the beginning of the service as a preparatory self-examination. The emphasis on sin and repentance, already strong in the middle ages, was reenforced by the Reformers. The first American Prayer Book of 1789 began the process of reducing the penitential emphasis by requiring the Ten Commandments only once a month and inserting the Summary of the Law as an alternative.

Kyrie, Trisagion, Gloria in Excelsis

The opening phase of the eucharist is concluded with one or more of three ancient hymns of praise.

"Kyrie eleison" or "Lord, have mercy" was a secular acclamation similar to the Jewish "Hosanna" (Save, Lord) or the English "God save the Queen" before it was adopted by Christians as a response to the petitions of a litany. In a brief threefold or ninefold pattern it became part of the mass, but was dropped from the second English Prayer Book and then restored in the American Prayer Book of 1789. Placed after the Summary of the Law it seems more like a prayer of penitence than one of praise. The 1979 Prayer Book restored the alternative of saying it in Greek (as it always was, even in the Latin mass), so allowing us to pray in the words and language of the very first Christians. In Greek, this is the oldest and most universal prayer in the whole liturgy.

The Trisagion ("Thrice Holy") comes from the Eastern Orthodox liturgy where it also serves as an entrance hymn.

The Gloria in excelsis has always been one of the most popular songs of praise, and often used at the beginning of the mass. The Gloria or some other hymn of praise must be used at Christmas and Easter and is always sung or said standing.

Thou that takes away the sins of the world,
  receive our prayer.
Thou that sittest at the right hand of God the Father,
  have mercy upon us.

For thou only art holy;
thou only art the Lord;
thou only, O Christ,
  with the Holy Ghost,
  art most high in the glory of God the Father. Amen.

The Collect of the Day

The Celebrant says to the people

> The Lord be with you.
> *People*   And with thy spirit.
> *Celebrant* Let us pray.

The Celebrant says the Collect.

People   Amen.

The Lessons

The people sit. One or two Lessons, as appointed, are read, the Reader first saying

A Reading (Lesson) from _____ .

A citation giving chapter and verse may be added.

After each Reading, the Reader may say

> The Word of the Lord.
> *People*   Thanks be to God.

or the Reader may say   Here endeth the Reading (Epistle).

The Collect of the Day

The readings for the day are now introduced with a theme prayer that sets the tone for the day. In effect, it "collects" our thoughts around a central theme that the Readings will develop. There are separate collects provided for every Sunday and Holy Day of the Christian Year, as well as for weddings and funerals and other special occasions.

The Lessons

In the early days of the church, the Scriptures were read "as long as time permits," but gradually a pattern was established so that certain lessons were always read on particular occasions. In recent years, Roman Catholics, Anglicans, and others have adopted a three-year cycle of readings that reflect the seasons and special days of the Church Year. Three lessons are normally read, one from the Old Testament, one from the Epistles, and one from the Gospels. In Easter Season, a reading from the Book of Acts or Revelation may take the place of the Old Testament reading. The Old Testament reading is often chosen for its relationship to the Gospel, but the Epistles and Gospels are usually read in a continuous sequence from week to week. The first two readings may be read by members of the congregation, but the Gospel must be read by someone who has been ordained. Because the Gospel gives us either the words or actions of Christ, it is given special honor. All stand and turn toward the Gospel book, which is often carried into the middle of the congregation and sometimes accompanied by acolytes carrying torches and a cross. Psalms, hymns, other music, and periods of silence may separate the readings to allow the readers to move to the place from which they will read and to allow the congregation opportunity to meditate on the words they have heard. Responses are also provided after the lessons and before and after the Gospel.

Silence may follow.

A Psalm, hymn, or anthem may follow each Reading.

Then, all standing, the Deacon or a Priest reads the Gospel, first saying

The Holy Gospel of our Lord Jesus Christ
according to _____ .

People   Glory be to thee, O Lord.

After the Gospel, the Reader says

The Gospel of the Lord.

People   Praise be to thee, O Christ.

The Sermon

On Sundays and other Major Feasts there follows, all standing

The Nicene Creed

We believe in one God,
   the Father, the Almighty,
   maker of heaven and earth,
   of all that is, seen and unseen.

We believe in one Lord, Jesus Christ,
   the only Son of God,
   eternally begotten of the Father,
   God from God, Light from Light,
   true God from true God,
   begotten, not made,
   of one Being with the Father.
   Through him all things were made.
   For us and for our salvation
      he came down from heaven:

The Sermon

The readings from the Bible are followed by a sermon based on the readings, which proclaims the Word, points out its relationship to our lives, and urges us to live by its light.

The Nicene Creed

The congregation now responds to the Word of God by affirming its belief in the words of the Nicene Creed. This great summary of the Christian faith was drawn up by the Council of Nicaea in A.D.325 (and slightly modified by later councils). As a statement of what the church believes, it appropriately begins with the word *We*. The Latin church changed the *We* to *I*, and that form was used in the Prayer Book until the present revision.

The Prayers of the People

Now the direction of the service changes and we begin to move toward God with our needs, failures, and gifts. First, we bring our needs and offer them to God. The Intercession is like an offering basket in which we place our individual concerns: for the church, its ministry, its members; for our leaders, for social responsibility; and, finally, for those in particular need and for the departed. One or several individuals may lead this prayer. A response to each paragraph may be made, and brief pauses may allow time for silent prayer. Opportunity may also be given for individuals to name their own concerns. The alternative prayers in Rite II may also be used.

Confession of Sin

Two Exhortations are provided: the longer one provides a useful prescription for confession: true repentance, love toward others, and intention for the future.

Like the Intercession, the Confession is stated in general terms but should be filled out with our own needs: the failures, individual and social, that weigh on us, which we need to turn over to God.

The Absolution balances the Exhortation: pardon for repentance, new strength for our love, and eternal life for our future. Their emphasis on Scripture led the sixteenth century Reformers to buttress the

by the power of the Holy Spirit
  he became incarnate from the Virgin Mary,
  and was made man.
For our sake he was crucified under Pontius Pilate;
  he suffered death and was buried.
    On the third day he rose again
      in accordance with the Scriptures;
    he ascended into heaven
      and is seated at the right hand of the Father.
He will come again in glory to judge the living and the dead,
  and his kingdom will have no end.

We believe in the Holy Spirit, the Lord, the giver of life,
  who proceeds from the Father and the Son.
  With the Father and the Son he is worshiped and glorified.
  He has spoken through the Prophets.
  We believe in one holy catholic and apostolic Church.
  We acknowledge one baptism for the forgiveness of sins.
  We look for the resurrection of the dead,
    and the life of the world to come. Amen.

or this

I believe in one God,
  the Father Almighty,
  maker of heaven and earth,
  and of all things visible and invisible;

And in one Lord Jesus Christ,
  the only-begotten Son of God,
  begotten of his Father before all worlds,
  God of God, Light of Light,
  very God of very God,
  begotten, not made,
  being of one substance with the Father;
  by whom all things were made;

who for us men and for our salvation
    came down from heaven,
and was incarnate by the Holy Ghost of the Virgin Mary,
    and was made man;
and was crucified also for us under Pontius Pilate;
he suffered and was buried;
and the third day he rose again according to the Scriptures,
and ascended into heaven,
and sitteth on the right hand of the Father;
and he shall come again, with glory,
    to judge both the quick and the dead;
whose kingdom shall have no end.

And I believe in the Holy Ghost the Lord, and Giver of Life,
    who proceedeth from the Father and the Son;
    who with the Father and the Son together is worshiped
        and glorified;
    who spake by the Prophets.
And I believe one holy Catholic and Apostolic Church;
I acknowledge one Baptism for the remission of sins;
and I look for the resurrection of the dead,
    and the life of the world to come. Amen.

The Prayers of the People

*Intercession is offered according to the following form, or in accordance
with the directions on page 383.*

The Deacon or other person appointed says

Let us pray for the whole state of Christ's Church and the
world.

*After each paragraph of this prayer, the People may make an appropriate
response, as directed.*

Almighty and everliving God, who in thy holy Word hast taught us to make prayers, and supplications, and to give thanks for all men: Receive these our prayers which we offer unto thy divine Majesty, beseeching thee to inspire continually the Universal Church with the spirit of truth, unity, and concord; and grant that all those who do confess thy holy Name may agree in the truth of thy holy Word, and live in unity and godly love.

Give grace, O heavenly Father, to all bishops and other ministers [especially _____], that they may, both by their life and doctrine, set forth thy true and lively Word, and rightly and duly administer thy holy Sacraments.

And to all thy people give thy heavenly grace, and especially to this congregation here present; that, with meek heart and due reverence, they may hear and receive thy holy Word, truly serving thee in holiness and righteousness all the days of their life.

We beseech thee also so to rule the hearts of those who bear the authority of government in this and every land [especially _____], that they may be led to wise decisions and right actions for the welfare and peace of the world.

Open, O Lord, the eyes of all people to behold thy gracious hand in all thy works, that, rejoicing in thy whole creation, they may honor thee with their substance, and be faithful stewards of thy bounty.

And we most humbly beseech thee, of thy goodness, O Lord, to comfort and succor [_____ and] all those who, in this transitory life, are in trouble, sorrow, need, sickness, or any other adversity.

Additional petitions and thanksgivings may be included here.

And we also bless thy holy Name for all thy servants
departed this life in thy faith and fear [especially _____],
beseeching thee to grant them continual growth in thy love
and service; and to grant us grace so to follow the good
examples of [_____ and of] all thy saints, that with
them we may be partakers of thy heavenly kingdom.

Grant these our prayers, O Father, for Jesus Christ's sake,
our only Mediator and Advocate. *Amen.*

*If there is no celebration of the Communion, or if a priest is not available,
the service is concluded as directed on page 406.*

Confession of Sin

*A Confession of Sin is said here if it has not been said earlier. On
occasion, the Confession may be omitted.*

*The Deacon or Celebrant says the following, or else the Exhortation
on page 316*

Ye who do truly and earnestly repent you of your sins, and
are in love and charity with your neighbors, and intend to
lead a new life, following the commandments of God, and
walking from henceforth in his holy ways: Draw near with
faith, and make your humble confession to Almighty God,
devoutly kneeling.

or this

Let us humbly confess our sins unto Almighty God.

Silence may be kept.

Minister and People

Almighty God,
Father of our Lord Jesus Christ,
maker of all things, judge of all men:
We acknowledge and bewail our manifold sins
    and wickedness,
which we from time to time most grievously have committed,
by thought, word, and deed, against thy divine Majesty,
provoking most justly thy wrath and indignation against us.
We do earnestly repent,
and are heartily sorry for these our misdoings;
the remembrance of them is grievous unto us,
the burden of them is intolerable.
Have mercy upon us,
have mercy upon us, most merciful Father;
for thy Son our Lord Jesus Christ's sake,
forgive us all that is past;
and grant that we may ever hereafter
serve and please thee in newness of life,
to the honor and glory of thy Name;
through Jesus Christ our Lord. Amen.

or this

Most merciful God,
we confess that we have sinned against thee
in thought, word, and deed,
by what we have done,
and by what we have left undone.
We have not loved thee with our whole heart;
we have not loved our neighbors as ourselves.
We are truly sorry and we humbly repent.
For the sake of thy Son Jesus Christ,
have mercy on us and forgive us;
that we may delight in thy will,
and walk in thy ways,
to the glory of thy Name. Amen.

Absolution with citations from the Bible. These four quotations invite, re-assure, and promise, as they tell us that God sent Jesus as an expression of love, to save us from our sins, and to intercede for us eternally.

The Peace
St. Paul urged the Corinthian Christians to "Greet one another with a holy kiss" (2 Corinthians 13:12) and a physical expression of our unity in Christ seems to have been part of the eucharist from the earliest times. There is a fine line to be drawn here between too little and too much, between a natural expression of love and joy—and an interruption in the flow of the service.

The Holy Communion

The Offertory
As we have brought our needs and sins before God, so now we offer symbols of our lives and our work: money, bread, and wine. This also has been part of the liturgy from the earliest times. Members of the congregation came forward to offer their bread and wine for the altar and for the needy. The "Offertory Procession" expresses our offering of our selves in God's service. A hymn or anthem may be sung while this offering is made and the altar is prepared.

The Great Thanksgiving
The central prayer of the eucharist begins with a dialogue called the Sursum corda which is often sung. It has been said that the Great Thanksgiving is "as much a hymn as a prayer." As in a hymn, we are praising God and giving thanks for all God has done through Jesus Christ for us.

The Bishop when present, or the Priest, stands and says

Almighty God, our heavenly Father, who of his great mercy hath promised forgiveness of sins to all those who with hearty repentance and true faith turn unto him, have mercy upon you, pardon and deliver you from all your sins, confirm and strengthen you in all goodness, and bring you to everlasting life; through Jesus Christ our Lord. *Amen.*

A Minister may then say one or more of the following sentences, first saying

Hear the Word of God to all who truly turn to him.

Come unto me, all ye that travail and are heavy laden, and I will refresh you.   *Matthew 11:28*

God so loved the world, that he gave his only-begotten Son, to the end that all that believe in him should not perish, but have everlasting life.   *John 3:16*

This is a true saying, and worthy of all men to be received, that Christ Jesus came into the world to save sinners.
1 Timothy 1:15

If any man sin, we have an Advocate with the Father, Jesus Christ the righteous; and he is the perfect offering for our sins, and not for ours only, but for the sins of the whole world.   *1 John 2:1-2*

The Peace

All stand. The Celebrant says to the people

> The peace of the Lord be always with you.

People   And with thy spirit.

Then the Ministers and People may greet one another in the name of the Lord.

The Holy Communion

The Celebrant may begin the Offertory with one of the sentences on pages 343-344, or with some other sentence of Scripture.

During the Offertory, a hymn, psalm, or anthem may be sung.

Representatives of the congregation bring the people's offerings of bread and wine, and money or other gifts, to the deacon or celebrant. The people stand while the offerings are presented and placed on the Altar.

The Great Thanksgiving

An alternative form will be found on page 340.

Eucharistic Prayer I

The people remain standing. The Celebrant, whether bishop or priest, faces them and sings or says

        The Lord be with you.
People   And with thy spirit.
Celebrant Lift up your hearts.
People   We lift them up unto the Lord.
Celebrant Let us give thanks unto our Lord God.
People   It is meet and right so to do.

Then, facing the Holy Table, the Celebrant proceeds

It is very meet, right, and our bounden duty, that we should at all times, and in all places, give thanks unto thee, O Lord, holy Father, almighty, everlasting God.

Here a Proper Preface is sung or said on all Sundays, and on other occasions as appointed.

Therefore with Angels and Archangels, and with all the company of heaven, we laud and magnify thy glorious Name; evermore praising thee, and saying,

Celebrant and People

Holy, holy, holy, Lord God of Hosts:
Heaven and earth are full of thy glory.
Glory be to thee, O Lord Most High.

Here may be added

Blessed is he that cometh in the name of the Lord.
Hosanna in the highest.

The people kneel or stand.

Then the Celebrant continues

All glory be to thee, Almighty God, our heavenly Father, for that thou, of thy tender mercy, didst give thine only Son Jesus Christ to suffer death upon the cross for our redemption; who made there, by his one oblation of himself once offered, a full, perfect, and sufficient sacrifice, oblation, and satisfaction, for the sins of the whole world; and did institute, and in his holy Gospel command us to continue, a perpetual memory of that his precious death and sacrifice, until his coming again.

At the following words concerning the bread, the Celebrant is to hold it, or lay a hand upon it; and at the words concerning the cup, to hold or place a hand upon the cup and any other vessel containing wine to be consecrated.

For in the night in which he was betrayed, he took bread; and when he had given thanks, he brake it, and gave it to his

The Sursum corda is usually followed by a proper preface (see pages 344-349). These are brief statements of particular cause for thanksgiving, such as the celebration of Christmas, Easter, a saint's day, a special occasion, or Sunday.

The preface leads into the Sanctus, a song sung by angels in Isaiah's vision of heaven (Isaiah 6.3), and the Benedictus qui venit, the song with which Jesus was welcomed into Jerusalem (Matthew 21.9) and which looks forward to his coming among us now and at the end of time. These hymns unite us in praise as we begin the eucharistic prayer.

In the early church, this prayer was extemporaneous; an early record says the priest prayed "to the best of his ability." Gradually, however, a set pattern evolved, and various prayers followed that pattern in different ways. The Western church has placed more emphasis on Jesus' death and the words of institution, while the Eastern church has focussed on the sanctifying action of the Holy Spirit. The Episcopal Church followed a Scottish pattern that incorporated the Eastern invocation of the Holy Spirit. Thus the prayer begins by giving God glory for the gift of Jesus Christ and his death for us and then recalls specifically Jesus' words and acts at the Last Supper. The Words of Institution are followed by the Oblation, in which we offer the gifts that represent Christ's sacrifice, his death, resurrection, and ascension. We then invoke God's Word and Holy Spirit to sanctify the bread and wine so that we, receiving them, may receive the Body and Blood of Christ. Three brief concluding paragraphs ask acceptance of our offering, unity in Christ, and forgiveness of our sins. The prayer ends with the great AMEN, capitalized for emphasis, which expresses our assent to the words said on our behalf in this central act of worship.

As we began this prayer in dialogue and unison, so we end it reciting the Lord's Prayer in unison. This prayer sums up what we are doing: hallowing God's Name, receiving a foretaste of the kingdom, being fed, being forgiven, being delivered from the power of evil, and ascribing all glory to the loving God who has taught us how to pray.

disciples, saying, "Take, eat, this is my Body, which is given for you. Do this in remembrance of me."

Likewise, after supper, he took the cup; and when he had given thanks, he gave it to them, saying, "Drink ye all of this; for this is my Blood of the New Testament, which is shed for you, and for many, for the remission of sins. Do this, as oft as ye shall drink it, in remembrance of me."

Wherefore, O Lord and heavenly Father, according to the institution of thy dearly beloved Son our Savior Jesus Christ, we, thy humble servants, do celebrate and make here before thy divine Majesty, with these thy holy gifts, which we now offer unto thee, the memorial thy Son hath commanded us to make; having in remembrance his blessed passion and precious death, his mighty resurrection and glorious ascension; rendering unto thee most hearty thanks for the innumerable benefits procured unto us by the same.

And we most humbly beseech thee, O merciful Father, to hear us; and, of thy almighty goodness, vouchsafe to bless and sanctify, with thy Word and Holy Spirit, these thy gifts and creatures of bread and wine; that we, receiving them according to thy Son our Savior Jesus Christ's holy institution, in remembrance of his death and passion, may be partakers of his most blessed Body and Blood.

And we earnestly desire thy fatherly goodness mercifully to accept this our sacrifice of praise and thanksgiving; most humbly beseeching thee to grant that, by the merits and death of thy Son Jesus Christ, and through faith in his blood, we, and all thy whole Church, may obtain remission of our sins, and all other benefits of his passion.

And here we offer and present unto thee, O Lord, our selves, our souls and bodies, to be a reasonable, holy, and living sacrifice unto thee; humbly beseeching thee that we, and all others who shall be partakers of this Holy Communion, may worthily receive the most precious Body and Blood of thy Son Jesus Christ, be filled with thy grace and heavenly benediction, and made one body with him, that he may dwell in us, and we in him.

And although we are unworthy, through our manifold sins, to offer unto thee any sacrifice, yet we beseech thee to accept this our bounden duty and service, not weighing our merits, but pardoning our offenses, through Jesus Christ our Lord;

By whom, and with whom, in the unity of the Holy Ghost all honor and glory be unto thee, O Father Almighty, world without end. *AMEN.*

And now, as our Savior Christ hath taught us, we are bold to say,

People and Celebrant

Our Father, who art in heaven,
    hallowed be thy Name,
    thy kingdom come,
    thy will be done,
        on earth as it is in heaven.
Give us this day our daily bread.
And forgive us our trespasses,
    as we forgive those who trespass against us.
And lead us not into temptation,
    but deliver us from evil.
For thine is the kingdom, and the power, and the glory,
    for ever and ever. Amen.

The Breaking of the Bread

The Celebrant breaks the consecreted Bread.

A period of silence is kept.

Then may be sung or said

[Alleluia.] Christ our Passover is sacrificed for us;
Therefore let us keep the feast. [*Alleluia.*]

*In Lent, Alleluia is omitted, and may be omitted at other times except
during Easter Season.*

The following or some other suitable anthem may be sung or said here

O Lamb of God, that takest away the sins of the world,
have mercy upon us.
O Lamb of God, that takest away the sins of the world,
have mercy upon us.
O Lamb of God, that takest away the sins of the world,
grant us thy peace.

*The following prayer may be said. The People may join in saying
this prayer*

We do not presume to come to this thy Table, O merciful
Lord, trusting in our own righteousness, but in thy manifold
and great mercies. We are not worthy so much as to gather
up the crumbs under thy Table. But thou art the same Lord
whose property is always to have mercy. Grant us therefore,
gracious Lord, so to eat the flesh of thy dear Son Jesus Christ,
and to drink his blood, that we may evermore dwell in him,
and he in us. *Amen.*

The Breaking of the Bread
Jesus made himself known to his disciples after the resurrection in the breaking of the bread (Luke 24.35), an action so distinctive that its description seems to have been the first title of the eucharist (see Acts 2:42). Whether a loaf of bread or "priest's host" is used, this action is still a critical moment in the service. The bread is broken as Christ's body was broken on the cross so that all might share the gift of forgiveness and new life. Silence and a brief optional dialogue (from I Corinthians 5:7-8) mark the Breaking of the Bread.

The Communion
In the middle ages, communion was received so rarely that it became separated from the mass and surrounded with its own devotions. The Reformers restored communion as an integral part of the mass but still provided devotions such as the Agnus Dei, the Prayer of Humble Access, and the Postcommunion Prayer. There are many ways in which communion is received: kneeling at an altar rail or standing at a communion station, receiving the bread in the hands or on the tongue, drinking from the chalice or "intincting" the wafer in the wine. Those ministering the sacrament will usually accommodate the individual's preference.

The postcommunion prayer, like the prayer before communion, was written by Archbishop Cranmer. It is a remarkable summary of the meaning of the eucharist: assurance of God's love, incorporation in Christ, a foretaste of the kingdom, and grace to serve Christ now.

Blessing and Dismissal
Archbishop Cranmer composed the Blessing by adding a verse from the Epistle to the Philippians (4:7) to the old Episcopal Blessing (the second form provided). The dismissal sends us out to do the work to which we are called and for which we have now been strengthened by Christ's life in ours.

Facing the people, the Celebrant may say the following Invitation

The Gifts of God for the People of God

and may add   Take them in remembrance that Christ died for
            you, and feed on him in your hearts by faith,
            with thanksgiving.

*The ministers receive the Sacrament in both kinds, and then immediately
deliver it to the people.*

The Bread and the Cup are given to the communicants with these words

The Body of our Lord Jesus Christ, which was given for thee,
preserve thy body and soul unto everlasting life. Take and eat
this in remembrance that Christ died for thee, and feed on
him in thy heart by faith, with thanksgiving.

The Blood of our Lord Jesus Christ, which was shed for thee,
preserve thy body and soul unto everlasting life. Drink this in
remembrance that Christ's Blood was shed for thee, and be
thankful.

or with these words

The Body (Blood) of our Lord Jesus Christ keep you in
everlasting life. [*Amen.*]

or with these words

The Body of Christ, the bread of heaven. [*Amen.*]
The Blood of Christ, the cup of salvation. [*Amen.*]

*During the ministration of Communion, hymns, psalms, or anthems may
be sung.*

*When necessary, the Celebrant consecrates additional bread and wine,
using the form on page 408.*

Let us pray.

The People may join in saying this prayer

Almighty and everliving God, we most heartily thank thee
for that thou dost feed us, in these holy mysteries, with the
spiritual food of the most precious Body and Blood of thy
Son our Savior Jesus Christ; and dost assure us thereby of
thy favor and goodness towards us; and that we are very
members incorporate in the mystical body of thy Son, the
blessed company of all faithful people; and are also heirs,
through hope, of thy everlasting kingdom. And we humbly
beseech thee, O heavenly Father, so to assist us with thy
grace, that we may continue in that holy fellowship, and do
all such good works as thou hast prepared for us to walk in;
through Jesus Christ our Lord, to whom, with thee and the
Holy Ghost, be all honor and glory, world without end.
Amen.

The Bishop when present, or the Priest, gives the blessing

The peace of God, which passeth all understanding, keep
your hearts and minds in the knowledge and love of God,
and of his Son Jesus Christ our Lord; and the blessing of
God Almighty, the Father, the Son, and the Holy Ghost, be
amongst you, and remain with you always. *Amen.*

or this

The blessing of God Almighty, the Father, the Son, and the
Holy Spirit, be upon you and remain with you for ever. *Amen.*

The Deacon, or the Celebrant, may dismiss the people with these words

      Let us go forth in the name of Christ.
People   Thanks be to God.

or the following

Deacon	Go in peace to love and serve the Lord.
People	Thanks be to God.

or this

Deacon	Let us go forth into the world, rejoicing in the power of the Spirit.
People	Thanks be to God.

or this

Deacon	Let us bless the Lord.
People	Thanks be to God.

From the Easter Vigil through the Day of Pentecost "Alleluia, alleluia" may be added to any of the dismissals.

The People respond Thanks be to God. Alleluia, alleluia.

Alternative Form
of the Great Thanksgiving

Eucharistic Prayer II

The people remain standing. The Celebrant, whether bishop or priest, faces them and sings or says

	The Lord be with you.
People	And with thy spirit.
Celebrant	Lift up your hearts.
People	We lift them up unto the Lord.
Celebrant	Let us give thanks unto our Lord God.
People	It is meet and right so to do.

The Holy Eucharist
Rite II

The same General Convention which approved the 1928 version of the Book of Common Prayer also created a Standing Liturgical Commission to begin work on the next revision. It was recognized that a deeper understanding of the early church and a closer relationship with other liturgical churches was rapidy creating a need for a more thorough revision. That revision, adopted in 1979, is Rite II. Rite I is a re-ordered and slightly reworded revision of the 1928 Prayer Book. The differences between them have been discussed already on page 6.

Rite II, like Rite I, can begin either with or without the Penitential Order. Most churches provide a printed order of service to give guidance on matters like this and on the hymns and service music to be found in the Hymnal.

A Penitential Order: Rite Two

For use at the beginning of the Liturgy, or as a separate service.

A hymn, psalm, or anthem may be sung.

The people standing, the Celebrant says

Blessed be God: Father, Son, and Holy Spirit.
People And blessed be his kingdom, now and for ever.
Amen.

In place of the above, from Easter Day through the Day of Pentecost

Celebrant Alleluia. Christ is risen.
People The Lord is risen indeed. Alleluia.

In Lent and on other penitential occasions

Celebrant Bless the Lord who forgives all our sins.
People His mercy endures for ever.

When used as a separate service, the Exhortation, page 316, may be read, or a homily preached.

The Decalogue may be said, the people kneeling.

The Celebrant may read one of the following sentences

Jesus said, "The first commandment is this: Hear, O Israel: The Lord our God is the only Lord. Love the Lord your God with all your heart, with all your soul, with all your mind, and with all your strength. The second is this: Love your neighbor as yourself. There is no other commandment greater than these." *Mark 12:29-31*

Before the Service Begins

Every church service involves a balance between what we do together and what we do as individuals. In that sense, we begin our worship as soon as we enter the church. In fact, even our going to church is an act of worship. We can use the time before the service begins to prepare ourselves for what we are about to do with others by simply sitting or kneeling and letting our minds become quiet and centered. We can also speak to God in our own words about the reasons we are here and what we hope to do. It can also be helpful to read quietly psalms such as Psalms 42 and 43 (pages 643-645).

A Penitential Order: Rite II

When we come into God's presence, we can appropriately respond with either praise or penitence as we emphasize either God's greatness or our unworthiness. It is appropriate sometimes to do one and sometimes the other. The Penitential Order is most often used to begin the service in Lent, but may be used at other times also or as a separate service. If it is not used at the beginning, the Confession of Sin will normally be said later in the service.

The Entrance and Salutation

See the discussion on page 18.

Words of Scripture

Prayer Book worship is always Biblical. The First English Prayer Book inserted the "Comfortable Words" of Scripture (still found in Rite I) into the eucharist after the confession and absolution as evidence of God's forgiveness. Here one or more passages of Scripture come before the confession. The Decalogue may be read here as a summary of God's will for us in our relationships with God and with each other. Three other passages of Scripture are provided. The first sets before us God's standard of love by which we are judged, the second promises forgiveness, and the third assures us that God's forgiveness is accessible to us, since Jesus, who shares our human nature and died for us, is the one who sits on "the throne of grace."

If we say that we have no sin, we deceive ourselves, and the truth is not in us. But if we confess our sins, God, who is faithful and just, will forgive our sins and cleanse us from all unrighteousness.   *1 John 1:8, 9*

Since we have a great high priest who has passed through the heavens, Jesus, the Son of God, let us with confidence draw near to the throne of grace, that we may receive mercy and find grace to help in time of need.   *Hebrews 4:14, 16*

The Deacon or Celebrant then says

Let us confess our sins against God and our neighbor.

Silence may be kept.

Minister and People

Most merciful God,
we confess that we have sinned against you
in thought, word, and deed,
by what we have done,
and by what we have left undone.
We have not loved you with our whole heart;
we have not loved our neighbors as ourselves.
We are truly sorry and we humbly repent.
For the sake of your Son Jesus Christ,
have mercy on us and forgive us;
that we may delight in your will,
and walk in your ways,
to the glory of your Name. Amen.

The Confession and Absolution

Sin has been defined most simply as separation. We have a sense of separation from God and from other human beings. All religion is based on that sense of alienation and the need to overcome it. Sacrificial systems build on the idea that we can recover our unity by giving God something we value. Christians understand that there is nothing we can offer God, but that if we confess our sins, we will be forgiven. God in Christ has already offered his own life to God on our behalf to restore our unity; we need only admit our need and accept in thankfulness what God in Christ has done.

The wording of the Confession is based on a contemporary English prayer, though some of the language goes back to the form of preparation said by the priest and acolyte before Mass in the Middle Ages. The Absolution is closely related to that form and was part of the Sarum Rite in England before the Reformation.

The Bishop when present, or the Priest, stands and says

Almighty God have mercy on you, forgive you all your sins through our Lord Jesus Christ, strengthen you in all goodness, and by the power of the Holy Spirit keep you in eternal life. *Amen.*

A deacon or lay person using the preceding form substitutes "us" for "you" and "our" for "your."

When this Order is used at the beginning of the Liturgy, the service continues with the Gloria in excelsis, the Kyrie eleison, or the Trisagion.

When used separately, it concludes with suitable prayers, and the Grace or a blessing.

The bishop or priest pronounces the Absolution, declaring our forgiveness. St. John's gospel tells us that Jesus gave his disciples authority to forgive sins immediately after his resurrection (St. John 20:22-23). The ordination service (on page 531) lists the declaration of absolution as a specific duty of priests.

Notice the sequence of verbs: *have mercy*: God begins the reconciling action by having compassion for us; *forgive*: God acts to remove the barriers we have created; *strengthen*: God acts to build up our resistance to sin and our ability to serve God; *keep*: God acts to hold us in a way of life that will keep us within the realm of God's love forever.

If the service begins with the Penitential Order, it moves now to one of the acts of praise on page 356.

The Holy Eucharist: Rite Two

The Word of God

A hymn, psalm, or anthem may be sung.

The people standing, the Celebrant says

              Blessed be God: Father, Son, and Holy Spirit.
People   And blessed be his kingdom, now and for ever.
              Amen.

In place of the above, from Easter Day through the Day of Pentecost

Celebrant Alleluia. Christ is risen.
People   The Lord is risen indeed. Alleluia.

In Lent and on other penitential occasions

Celebrant Bless the Lord who forgives all our sins.
People   His mercy endures for ever.

The Celebrant may say

Almighty God, to you all hearts are open, all desires known, and from you no secrets are hid: Cleanse the thoughts of our hearts by the inspiration of your Holy Spirit, that we may perfectly love you, and worthily magnify your holy Name; through Christ our Lord. *Amen.*

The Entrance

Those providing leadership for the service can enter during a hymn or simply walk to their places. Either way, it is customary for the congregation to stand. From the earliest times, a psalm, hymn, or anthem such as the Gloria or the Kyrie was used for the opening of the liturgy.

The Salutation

Every act of worship involves a conversation among those taking part as well as a conversation with God. The Salutation begins the service by drawing priest and people into a dialogue and establishing our reason for being here. Always we are here to praise God, but in Easter Season we praise God for raising Christ from the dead and in Lent and other penitential times we praise God who forgives our sins. The first salutation, "Blessed be God . . ." is based on Jewish custom and that of the Eastern church. The second salutation is the ancient Christian Easter greeting. The third salutation, based on Psalm 103:1-3 and 136:1-26, is used in Lent and on other penitential occasions.

The Collect for Purity

All Christian worship is Trinitarian, offered to God the Father in and through Jesus Christ by the power and inspiration of the Holy Spirit. The opening prayer, a hallmark of Anglican worship ever since the first English Prayer Book in 1549, sets this pattern clearly before us. Known as the "Collect for Purity," this prayer can be traced back to the eighth century; it was used in England before 1549 as a prayer said by the priest while vesting. Omission of this prayer is permitted and may allow the theme of praise to continue uninterrupted from the opening hymn through one of the first two salutations and into the Gloria in excelsis.

When appointed, the following hymn or some other song of praise is sung or said, all standing

Glory to God in the highest,
and peace to his people on earth.

Lord God, heavenly King,
almighty God and Father,
we worship you, we give you thanks,
we praise you for your glory.

Lord Jesus Christ, only Son of the Father,
Lord God, Lamb of God,
you take away the sin of the world:
have mercy on us;
you are seated at the right hand of the Father:
receive our prayer.

For you alone are the Holy One,
you alone are the Lord,
you alone are the Most High,
Jesus Christ,
with the Holy Spirit,
in the glory of God the Father. Amen.

On other occasions the following is used

Lord, have mercy.		Kyrie eleison.
Christ, have mercy.	*or*	*Christe eleison.*
Lord, have mercy.		Kyrie eleison.

or this

Holy God,
Holy and Mighty,
Holy Immortal One,
Have mercy upon us.

Acts of Praise

The opening movement of the service ends with one of three ancient Canticles or an alternative song of praise. Each of the choices provided can be traced almost to the beginnings of the church's life and has been used from very early times at this point in the eucharist. Christians seem to have felt instinctively that worship should begin with praise. These hymns enable us to join in praise with Christians from every time and place.

The Gloria in Excelsis

We do not know either the date or authorship of this Canticle but it was in use in the church from at least the fourth century. Gradually, it became a more frequent part of the eucharist until it became, as it is today, one of the most familiar parts of the service. The opening words are easily identified as the hymn the angels sang in announcing the birth of Christ to the shepherds. The second and fourth paragraphs have a striking resemblance to the Te Deum while the third paragraph is reminiscent of the Agnus Dei (O Lamb of God . . . have mercy upon us). This Canticle is, most simply put, a collection of "phrases of praises."

The Kyrie

Of equal age and significance, the Kyrie seems to be derived from the praise songs of earthly rulers. "Have mercy . . ." sounds to the modern ear like a plea for forgiveness, but like the Hebrew "Hosanna" and the English "God save the Queen," is simply a shout of praise. The Kyrie can be said or sung in English or, to unite us again with the very words of the early church, in the original Greek. Each phrase is often repeated three times.

The Trisagion

The third Canticle offered is a part of the liturgy of the Eastern church. Anglican liturgy has been influenced since the seventeenth century by the liturgy of the Eastern Orthodox Church, and that influence is especially strong in this Prayer Book. It is appropriate that our praise of God unite us with Christians of other times and places.

The Collect of the Day

The Celebrant says to the people

The Lord be with you.
People   **And also with you.**
Celebrant   **Let us pray.**

The Celebrant says the Collect.

People   **Amen.**

The Lessons

The people sit. One or two Lessons, as appointed, are read, the Reader first saying

A Reading (Lesson) from _____ .

A citation giving chapter and verse may be added.

After each Reading, the Reader may say

The Word of the Lord.
People   **Thanks be to God.**

or the Reader may say   **Here ends the Reading (Epistle).**

Silence may follow.

A Psalm, hymn, or anthem may follow each Reading.

Then, all standing, the Deacon or a Priest reads the Gospel, first saying

The Holy Gospel of our Lord Jesus Christ according to _____ .
People   **Glory to you, Lord Christ.**

Any of these Canticles may be simply recited in unison, sung to familiar music by the congregation, or sung by a choir with a more elaborate setting.

The Collect of the Day

The Collect is the "theme prayer" of the day, different for every Sunday and holy day, and is intended to *collect* (hence the name) the prayers of the congregation around a single subject. It was a normal part of the eucharist as early as the fifth or sixth century. Many of the collects are of medieval origin and were brilliantly re-cast in translation by Thomas Cranmer. Some—for example the great collect for the first Sunday in Advent—were Cranmer's own composition. His gift for language is evident here as, perhaps, nowhere else. The Rite II Collects can be found between pages 211 and 261.

The Lessons

A document from about A.D. 150 us that when Christians assemble for worship, "the memoirs of the Apostles or the writings of the prophets are read, as long as time permits." Gradually, of course, a more formal pattern had to be adopted, and it became customary to read selections from the Old Testament, the Gospels, and other parts of the New Testament in an annual sequence that enabled the church to include passages appropriate to particular seasons and celebrations. This pattern, developed in the early Middle Ages, continued almost unchanged until after the Second Vatican Council in the 1960s. As a result of that Council, the Roman Catholic Church developed a new three-year calendar of readings which many other churches have adapted to their own use.

The Gospel, since it is the record of what Jesus himself said or did, is always given the highest honor. Often there is a procession to carry the Gospel book to a prominent place in the church. The Gospel is always read by an ordained person (a deacon if there is one taking part in the service) while the congregation stands and turns, if necessary, toward the reader.

Psalms, hymns, or anthems are usually sung between the readings when the service includes music. If not, a psalm is usually read responsively or in unison. A period of silence is often kept after each reading to allow opportunity to reflect on what has been said.

> The Gospel of the Lord.
>
> *People*   Praise to you, Lord Christ.

The Sermon

On Sundays and other Major Feasts there follows, all standing

The Nicene Creed

We believe in one God,
   the Father, the Almighty,
   maker of heaven and earth,
   of all that is, seen and unseen.

We believe in one Lord, Jesus Christ,
   the only Son of God,
   eternally begotten of the Father,
   God from God, Light from Light,
   true God from true God,
   begotten, not made,
   of one Being with the Father.
   Through him all things were made.
For us and for our salvation
   he came down from heaven:
by the power of the Holy Spirit
   he became incarnate from the Virgin Mary,
   and was made man.
For our sake he was crucified under Pontius Pilate;
   he suffered death and was buried.
   On the third day he rose again
      in accordance with the Scriptures;
   he ascended into heaven
      and is seated at the right hand of the Father.

The Sermon

Preaching and communion are the two focal points of Christian worship. In some churches and at some times in history one has been exalted at the expense of the other, but both are essential and must be kept in balance if God's Word is to work in us fully. Thus in the first part of the liturgy it is the sermon that brings the Word of God to bear on our lives, and in the second part of the liturgy it is through the consecrated bread and wine that God's Word enters our lives. Ideally, the sermon is completely integrated into the liturgy and has three contact points: (1) the readings that provide the "text", (2) the liturgy itself, and (3) the congregation. The sermon takes the readings and applies them to our lives in the eucharistic context. The emphasis will vary, depending on the occasion, the preacher, and the congregation, but the sermon is always a means by which the Word of God is proclaimed to the people of God.

The Creed

The Nicene Creed is recited as our response to the Word that we have read and proclaimed. This Creed is the fullest statement of faith agreed to by all Christians from the earliest times. It was adopted by the Council of Nicaea in 325 and given its present form at the Council of Constantinople in 381. In earlier Prayer Books the Creed was presented as an individual statement of faith beginning with the words "I believe . . ." but the Councils originally drew it up as a corporate statement of all believers and began it with the plural form. Christians speaking together should logically say "We believe."

The reaffirmation of baptismal vows may take the place of the Creed on All Saints' Day or the Sunday after All Saints' Day, on the Feast of the Baptism of our Lord in January, and on the Day of Pentecost.

The Creed is both simple and subtle. It is, at the simplest level, a straightforward statement of belief in a Triune God who is Creator, Redeemer, and Sanctifier. Yet the subtleties of the Creed will repay careful study. Notice, for example, how the placement of a comma in the last line of the first paragraph prevents us from thinking that everything God has made is either seen or unseen. Much of God's creation, as any scientist knows, is not simply unseen, but unseeable.

He will come again in glory to judge the living and the dead,
and his kingdom will have no end.

We believe in the Holy Spirit, the Lord, the giver of life,
who proceeds from the Father and the Son.
With the Father and the Son he is worshiped and glorified.
He has spoken through the Prophets.
We believe in one holy catholic and apostolic Church.
We acknowledge one baptism for the forgiveness of sins.
We look for the resurrection of the dead,
and the life of the world to come. Amen.

The Prayers of the People

Prayer is offered with intercession for

The Universal Church, its members, and its mission
The Nation and all in authority
The welfare of the world
The concerns of the local community
Those who suffer and those in any trouble
The departed (with commemoration of a saint when appropriate)

See the forms beginning on page 383.

*If there is no celebration of the Communion, or if a priest is not available,
the service is concluded as directed on page 406.*

Confession of Sin

*A Confession of Sin is said here if it has not been said earlier. On
occasion, the Confession may be omitted.*

One of the sentences from the Penitential Order on page 351 may be said.

The placement of a comma preserves that possibility.

Then notice the line in the second paragraph that says "of one Being with the Father . . ." This was added to the Creed as a result of a fierce battle at the Council of Nicaea in A.D. 325. One side contended that Jesus was of *similar* being with God the Father while the other side held that Jesus was of the same essential nature. In Greek the difference is one letter (*homo-ousion* or *homoi-ousion*). But that letter makes all the difference. In Christ, we assert here, we are united with God's own essential being.

In the second line of the third paragraph, the words *and the Son* have been the center of controversy between Eastern Orthodox Christians and Western Catholic Christians. Some Episcopalians are willing to drop this phrase for the sake of closer ties with the Eastern church, but the subject is both difficult and delicate.

Finally, we should remember that worship shapes theology as well as the reverse. Theology attempts to put into words the knowledge of God we come to in worship, but worship always goes beyond theology. God's love of us and our love of God go beyond words. The Creed is more than theology; it is also a hymn of praise to the God who loves us. We can sing it as a hymn or explore the depths of its theology. Either way, it reminds us of God's greatness and glory and the wonder that such a God loves us so much.

The Prayers of the People

To pray for ourselves and others is one of the fundamental reasons we come to God. A deacon or lay person usually leads this prayer. Often there will be a method of collecting intercessions from individuals before the service begins; usually there will be pauses during the prayer when we can speak our particular intercessions, aloud or inwardly, so that in one way or another the intercession becomes a gathering and presenting of the concerns of the whole congregation. Six alternative forms for the Prayers of the People are given on pages 383 to 393, but the prayer leader may also write the prayer (following the guidelines on pages 359 and 383). Other forms in the Prayer Book, such as the Great Litany (page 148) or the Litany of Thanksgiving (page 836) may also be used on occasion.

The Prayers of the People (pages 383-395)

The offering of prayer is appropriately the freest part of the service since it should reflect the great variety of needs and concerns with which God's people come together. In many parishes a deacon or lay person is appointed to lead these prayers and often that person works with a committee to ensure that the congregation's concerns are expressed. The Prayer Book lists six areas of concern that should be included: the universal church, the nation and those in authority, the welfare of the world, the local community, those in suffering or trouble, and the departed.

Form I

One of the oldest forms of intercession is the litany, which allows a great many needs to be presented in short petitions and which calls for frequent response from the congregation. The Great Litany (pages 148 to 155) is probably the best-known examples. This prayer is modelled on Orthodox litanies of intercession. Note that additional intercessions may be inserted and that some petitions are marked for possible omission. The petition for absolution of sins need not be used if there is a confession otherwise included in the service.

Form II

Modern American Christians are not much used to silence, but it is encouraged by the 1979 Prayer Book and, as here, can provide opportunity for individual Christians to be united in common worship as each silently expresses the great variety of cares and concerns that each needs to offer. Form II is the simplest of the forms provided here and therefore the most flexible. It becomes what each Christian is able to make of it.

Form III

This form has a different kind of simplicity: responses are provided as the petitions move quickly through the six categories of prayer called for in the general directions for intercession. The prayer ends with an invitation to pray "for our own needs and those of others," which allows for either a silent or spoken response.

Form IV
These petitions, also, move quickly through the six categories suggested, but there is silence called for after each and an opportunity for members of the congregation to express their own concerns silently or aloud.

Form V
Like Form I, this is a litany with a response to be made (though, unlike Form I, the response is printed only after the first petition). Here, too, there is opportunity for special intercessions. The closing doxology links our prayer with the prayers for us of the Virgin Mary and other saints. If the parish church is dedicated to a particular saint, this doxology provides a place to mention that saint as well.

Form VI
Like Form III, this form moves quickly through petitions and response, but there is opportunity given to express particular thanksgivings and intercessions. The prayer is unique in closing with a form of confession. If Form VI is used, the Confession on page 360 would be omitted.

The Collect at the Prayers
For the closing collect, the priest can choose not only from the prayers on pages 394-395 but also from others that may better reflect the season or some special need of the congregation.

The eight collects illustrate the way in which the Prayer Book brings together prayers from a wide variety of sources. Prayers 1 and 6 are based on medieval prayers, while 2 and 4 are revised versions of prayers written by Thomas Cranmer in the sixteenth century. Prayer 5 comes from the Eastern Orthodox liturgies of St. Basil and St. John Chrysostom and goes back at least to the eighth century. Prayer 7 comes from modern Indian and African liturgies. Prayers 3 and 8 were written by twentieth century members of the Episcopal Church.

Prayer 6 is especially appropriate for Easter Season, Prayer 7 for Advent, and Prayer 8 for All Saints or other saint's days.

The Deacon or Celebrant says

Let us confess our sins against God and our neighbor.

Silence may be kept.

Minister and People

Most merciful God,
we confess that we have sinned against you
in thought, word, and deed,
by what we have done,
and by what we have left undone.
We have not loved you with our whole heart;
we have not loved our neighbors as ourselves.
We are truly sorry and we humbly repent.
For the sake of your Son Jesus Christ,
have mercy on us and forgive us;
that we may delight in your will,
and walk in your ways,
to the glory of your Name. Amen.

The Bishop when present, or the Priest, stands and says

Almighty God have mercy on you, forgive you all your sins
through our Lord Jesus Christ, strengthen you in all
goodness, and by the power of the Holy Spirit keep you in
eternal life. *Amen.*

The Peace

All stand. The Celebrant says to the people

> The peace of the Lord be always with you.

People   And also with you.

*Then the Ministers and People may greet one another in the
name of the Lord.*

Confession of Sin

The Confession may come at the beginning (see pages 351 to 353), as a preparation for the whole service, or here as a preparation for the act of communion. An alternative form of confession comes at the end of Intercession VI if that form is used.

As universal and instinctive as our need to pray is our need for forgiveness. To know God at all, is to know our failure to serve God perfectly. The bidding of the Confession reminds us that our sins separate us both from God and from our neighbor.

The Confession first notes that God is known to us from the beginning as a merciful God (cf. Exodus 34:6). We can confidently confess our sins knowing that God's very nature is forgiveness. We confess that by thought, word, and deed, by action and inaction, by failing to love God "with our whole heart" and "our neighbors as ourselves" we have fallen short of God's purpose for us.

Having examined the extent of our failure, we express our sorrow and repentance. We have no claim on God's forgiveness in ourselves, but in Christ we may dare to ask it so that we may be set free to delight in God's will and so that our lives may bring glory to God's Name.

The risen Christ gave his disciples authority to forgive sins in his Name. The importance of that act is underlined by the fact that the bishop, the successor of the apostles, will pronounce the absolution, if present. The words of the Absolution can be traced to the Sarum liturgy of medieval England. The Absolution reminds us that we have been given the gift of eternal life in baptism and need the help of the Holy Spirit to "keep" us in that life.

The Peace

Freed from sin, we are brought together in unity. The joy of that freedom and unity has been expressed from the earliest time in a ritual exchange. St. Paul exhorts those to whom he writes to "greet one another with a holy kiss." We are one body in Christ, knowing a unity deeper than words and needing some way to express that outwardly. The form of expression may vary from one congregation to another, but it is God's peace, human unity restored, that we celebrate here.

25

The Holy Communion

The Celebrant may begin the Offertory with one of the sentences on page 376, or with some other sentence of Scripture.

During the Offertory, a hymn, psalm, or anthem may be sung.

Representatives of the congregation bring the people's offerings of bread and wine, and money or other gifts, to the deacon or celebrant. The people stand while the offerings are presented and placed on the Altar.

The Great Thanksgiving

Alternative forms will be found on page 367 and following.

Eucharistic Prayer A

The people remain standing. The Celebrant, whether bishop or priest, faces them and sings or says

          The Lord be with you.
People   And also with you.
Celebrant Lift up your hearts.
People   We lift them to the Lord.
Celebrant Let us give thanks to the Lord our God.
People   It is right to give him thanks and praise.

Then, facing the Holy Table, the Celebrant proceeds

It is right, and a good and joyful thing, always and everywhere to give thanks to you, Father Almighty, Creator of heaven and earth.

Here a Proper Preface is sung or said on all Sundays, and on other occasions as appointed.

The Offertory

Early Christians brought their own bread and wine to be used at the eucharist. After it was brought forward to the deacons in an Offertory Procession, what was needed for the service was placed on the altar while the remainder was set aside for the needs of the poor. Since few of us make our own bread and wine anymore, these materials are provided from the money we offer, and both the bread and wine and the money are brought to the altar by representatives of the congregation.

If the parish has a deacon, it is the deacon who receives the offerings and then prepares the altar. From the bread brought forward, the right amount will be placed on the altar, and wine will be poured into the chalice. Acolytes may also assist in this preparation.

The words read to begin the Offertory are found on page 376. During the Offertory, a hymn or psalm may be sung or a choir may sing an anthem.

The Great Thanksgiving

(Alternative Eucharistic Prayers are provided on pages 367-375 of the Prayer Book and are discussed on page 32 of this book.)

The word *eucharist* means *thanksgiving* and reminds us that the central act of the service is the giving of thanks to God for all God's gifts to us. This focal prayer of the service begins with a dialogue between priest and congregation that comes from Jewish tradition. "Lift up your hearts" was a simple invitation to stand but the words take us beyond the physical to the emotional and spiritual. "Let us give thanks" asks the congregation to join in prayer. This dialogue is called the Sursum corda ("Let us lift hearts") and is often sung.

The invitation to pray is followed by a Preface which says that it is always right to give God thanks, and a Proper Preface, which provides a particular reason for giving thanks at each season of the year or special day or occasion. The Proper Prefaces can be found on pages 377-382.

Therefore we praise you, joining our voices with Angels and Archangels and with all the company of heaven, who for ever sing this hymn to proclaim the glory of your Name:

Celebrant and People

Holy, holy, holy Lord, God of power and might,
heaven and earth are full of your glory.
　Hosanna in the highest.
Blessed is he who comes in the name of the Lord.
　Hosanna in the highest.

The people stand or kneel.

Then the Celebrant continues

Holy and gracious Father: In your infinite love you made us for yourself; and, when we had fallen into sin and become subject to evil and death, you, in your mercy, sent Jesus Christ, your only and eternal Son, to share our human nature, to live and die as one of us, to reconcile us to you, the God and Father of all.

He stretched out his arms upon the cross, and offered himself, in obedience to your will, a perfect sacrifice for the whole world.

At the following words concerning the bread, the Celebrant is to hold it, or lay a hand upon it; and at the words concerning the cup, to hold or place a hand upon the cup and any other vessel containing wine to be consecrated.

On the night he was handed over to suffering and death, our Lord Jesus Christ took bread; and when he had given thanks to you, he broke it, and gave it to his disciples, and said, "Take, eat: This is my Body, which is given for you. Do this for the remembrance of me."

The Proper Preface and Preface end with an invitation to join in the Sanctus ("Holy"), a great hymn of praise that can be traced back to the Book of Isaiah (6:3) and Revelation (4:8), where it is sung by angels before God's throne. The last part of this hymn, the Benedictus qui venit ("Blessed is he who comes"), recalls the words shouted by the people of Jerusalem as Jesus entered the city on Palm Sunday. In this hymn, we join with "angels, and archangels, and all the company of heaven" in singing praise before God's throne and, at the same time, praise the Lord who comes to us in this act of worship.

After the Sanctus, the congregation may kneel or continue to stand as the bishop or priest begins the central part of the prayer of consecration. Three alternative prayers are provided on pages 367-375.

It was Jewish custom to give thanks to God for food before every meal. Since all creation belongs to God, it is only right to thank God for whatever part of it we take for our own enjoyment. Jewish prayers of thanksgiving bless God for creating the particular food being enjoyed, saying, for example: "Blessed be God who brought forth bread from the earth . . ." or "Blessed be God who created the fruit of the vine . . ." So, in this prayer, we recite what God has done for us by sending Jesus into the world. This prayer is very much like the Creed in remembering how Jesus lived and died in order to reunite us with God.

At the heart of the Prayer of Consecration are the Words of Institution, the narrative of the Last Supper, drawn almost word for word from the Biblical accounts in St. Luke (22:19-20) and St. Paul's first letter to the Corinthians (11:23-25). The tradition of the Western church has been that the recital of these words brought about Christ's presence in the bread and wine; therefore they were marked with special solemnity and bells were rung while the priest raised the bread and cup and genuflected. In the eastern tradition, the invocation of the Holy Spirit was understood as the critical moment. The American Book of Common Prayer has always included both these elements in its prayer and never attempted to define a moment of transformation. It is sufficient to know that in the offering of our prayer, Christ becomes present in the elements and the action of the liturgy.

After supper he took the cup of wine; and when he had given
thanks, he gave it to them, and said, "Drink this, all of you:
This is my Blood of the new Covenant, which is shed for you
and for many for the forgiveness of sins. Whenever you drink
it, do this for the remembrance of me."

Therefore we proclaim the mystery of faith:

Celebrant and People

Christ has died.
Christ is risen.
Christ will come again.

The Celebrant continues

We celebrate the memorial of our redemption, O Father, in
this sacrifice of praise and thanksgiving. Recalling his death,
resurrection, and ascension, we offer you these gifts.

Sanctify them by your Holy Spirit to be for your people the
Body and Blood of your Son, the holy food and drink of new
and unending life in him. Sanctify us also that we may faithfully
receive this holy Sacrament, and serve you in unity, constancy,
and peace; and at the last day bring us with all your saints
into the joy of your eternal kingdom.

All this we ask through your Son Jesus Christ. By him, and
with him, and in him, in the unity of the Holy Spirit all honor
and glory is yours, Almighty Father, now and for ever. *AMEN.*

And now, as our Savior	As our Savior Christ
Christ has taught us,	has taught us,
we are bold to say,	we now pray,

The *memory* of Christ's death and resurrection is a strong element in the eucharist and sometimes overshadows the reality of Christ's presence. Memory does not depend on absence; rather, memory is often triggered when someone's presence calls to mind all they have meant to us. So the two disciples on the road to Emmaus, believing Christ dead and buried, remembered him when he took bread in their presence and broke it. The Greek word *anamnesis* used in the Gospel stories of the Last Supper implies much more than a recalling of past events. Here the Creator of time transcends time to make us present in the Upper Room and at Calvary and to be present with us here and now.

In the middle of this prayer the congregation makes a response called an "Acclamation." The Acclamation in this prayer ties our praise of God to past, present, and future. It also illustrates the way in which Christians are being brought together across time and space by liturgical change since the Acclamation has been a feature of worship in the Orthodox Churches and was first introduced in modern liturgies by the Church of South India in the 1950s.

After the Acclamation comes a paragraph that speaks of "this sacrifice of praise and thanksgiving." The idea of sacrifice is too complex to explain fully here but is of central importance. Clearly the eucharist links us somehow to Christ's death on Calvary and that connection must be noted even if a full understanding remains beyond us and continues to divide Christians in the very action in which they should be most united.

The invocation of the Holy Spirit (or *epiclesis*) is also characteristic of Eastern Christianity. The seventeenth-century Scottish Prayer Book first brought it to the West. When the first American bishop was consecrated by Scottish bishops, he promised to add an epiclesis to the American Prayer Book. The form of this prayer links us to other Christian churches in Scotland and the East.

The eucharistic prayer ends with a Trinitarian formula: our prayer is offered to God the Father through Jesus Christ in unity with the Holy Spirit.

Notice that the AMEN is printed in capital letters. The people's response at this point is critical because the priest has been speaking for all. From the earliest times this AMEN has been stressed. It

People and Celebrant

Our Father, who art in heaven, hallowed be thy Name, thy kingdom come, thy will be done, on earth as it is in heaven. Give us this day our daily bread. And forgive us our trespasses, as we forgive those who trespass against us. And lead us not into temptation, but deliver us from evil. For thine is the kingdom, and the power, and the glory, for ever and ever. Amen.	Our Father in heaven, hallowed be your Name, your kingdom come, your will be done, on earth as in heaven. Give us today our daily bread. Forgive us our sins as we forgive those who sin against us. Save us from the time of trial, and deliver us from evil. For the kingdom, the power, and the glory are yours, now and for ever. Amen.

The Breaking of the Bread

The Celebrant breaks the consecrated Bread.

A period of silence is kept.

Then may be sung or said

[Alleluia.] Christ our Passover is sacrificed for us;
Therefore let us keep the feast. [*Alleluia.*]

In Lent, Alleluia is omitted, and may be omitted at other times except during Easter Season.

In place of, or in addition to, the preceding, some other suitable anthem may be used.

Facing the people, the Celebrant says the following Invitation

The Gifts of God for the People of God.

should be a strong, loud, and clear assent.

As the eucharistic prayer began with the involvement of the whole congregation in the Sursum corda and the Sanctus, so it ends with all joining in the Lord's Prayer. The Lord's Prayer has been included in the eucharist almost from the beginning of the church's life and was placed at the end of the prayer of consecration by Pope Gregory the Great at the end of the sixth century. It is appropriate here not only because it is the prayer Jesus himself taught his followers, but also because of its reference to "daily bread." The word for "daily" used here in Greek is a very unusual word and seems to point beyond the bread of ordinary life to the bread of the great final day. It might be read, "Give us this day the bread of that day."

The Lord's Prayer is found in this form in the Sermon on the Mount (Matthew 6:9-13) but the ending ("for thine is the kingdom," etc.) seems to have been added after Jesus' resurrection and has not always been included, yet it forms a fitting conclusion not only to the Lord's Prayer but to the prayer of consecration as well.

The "traditional" version of the Lord's Prayer goes back to the Great Bible of 1539 and is older even than the King James Version. The modern version comes from an International Ecumenical Committee on English Language Texts.

The Breaking of the Bread

This dramatic moment in the liturgy is marked primarily by silence. In silence, the bread, the Body of Christ, is broken, and it is broken both symbolically and literally for us. Bread must be broken to be shared and Christ's body was broken on the cross so that all might be redeemed. After a period of silence, a "Fraction Anthem" is usually said or sung. The Prayer Book provides a verse and response drawn from 1 Corinthians 5:7, but the *Agnus Dei* ("O Lamb of God") is frequently used in addition or in place of it.

The Invitation to Communion ("The Gifts of God for the People of God") comes from the liturgies of the Eastern church where the usual form is "Holy things for Holy people." The optional addition ("Take them in remembrance") has been part of Anglican Prayer Books since 1552 when it was a sentence used in administering communion.

29

and may add   Take them in remembrance that Christ died for you, and feed on him in your hearts by faith, with thanksgiving.

The ministers receive the Sacrament in both kinds, and then immediately deliver it to the people.

The Bread and the Cup are given to the communicants with these words

The Body (Blood) of our Lord Jesus Christ keep you in everlasting life. [*Amen.*]

or with these words

The Body of Christ, the bread of heaven. [*Amen.*]
The Blood of Christ, the cup of salvation. [*Amen.*]

During the ministration of Communion, hymns, psalms, or anthems may be sung.

When necessary, the Celebrant consecrates additional bread and wine, using the form on page 408.

After Communion, the Celebrant says

Let us pray.

Celebrant and People

Eternal God, heavenly Father,
you have graciously accepted us as living members
of your Son our Savior Jesus Christ,
and you have fed us with spiritual food
in the Sacrament of his Body and Blood.
Send us now into the world in peace,
and grant us strength and courage
to love and serve you
with gladness and singleness of heart;
through Christ our Lord. Amen.

or the following

Communion

Communion is the fourth and final action of the liturgy of the altar but, oddly, there is no title or subtitle in the Prayer Book for the communion itself. As God came to us in flesh and blood in Jesus of Nazareth, so now God comes to us here in the bread and wine.

In the early church, it was customary to stand for communion.; it still is the ordinary practice of the Eastern church. Kneeling became common in the Western church only in the late Middle Ages and seems to reflect the emphasis on human sinfulness that was dominant in that period. Today, it is no longer unusual in the Episcopal Church to stand around the altar or to come in procession to a "communion station." Those who are prefer to stand are, of course, always welcome to stand, and those unable to come forward need only speak to an usher to arrange for a priest or eucharistic minister to come to them. Customs for receiving communion differ but it is always proper to cross the right hand over the left and hold them up to receive the bread, and it is helpful to guide the chalice to your lips by taking the base in your hand. Those who prefer to receive communion on the tongue can do so, and those who prefer not to receive from the chalice (recovering alcoholics, for example) can leave the rail before the chalice is presented or simply indicate their preference by a slight nod or arms folded across the chest. Some parishes make separate provision for those who prefer to receive by "intinction," dipping the edge of the bread into the wine, but in most parishes either the minister intincts the wafer for you or allows you to do so yourself. All baptized persons are welcome at God's table.

There is normally a period of time before you go forward, and after you return, that can be used for preparation, thanksgiving, and meditation. It may be a time to think back over the readings or the sermon and to see yourself in Christ's presence and responding to his teaching.

Psalms, hymns, and choir anthems are often sung during the time of communion.

Almighty and everliving God,
we thank you for feeding us with the spiritual food
of the most precious Body and Blood
of your Son our Savior Jesus Christ;
and for assuring us in these holy mysteries
that we are living members of the Body of your Son,
and heirs of your eternal kingdom.
And now, Father, send us out
to do the work you have given us to.do,
to love and serve you
as faithful witnesses of Christ our Lord.
To him, to you, and to the Holy Spirit,
be honor and glory, now and for ever. Amen.

The Bishop when present, or the Priest, may bless the people.

The Deacon, or the Celebrant, dismisses them with these words

> Let us go forth in the name of Christ.

People   Thanks be to God.

or this

Deacon   Go in peace to love and serve the Lord.
People   Thanks be to God.

or this

Deacon   Let us go forth into the world,
rejoicing in the power of the Spirit.
People   Thanks be to God.

or this

Deacon   Let us bless the Lord.
People   Thanks be to God.

From the Easter Vigil through the Day of Pentecost "Alleluia, alleluia" may be added to any of the dismissals.

The People respond   Thanks be to God. Alleluia, alleluia.

After Communion

In the early days of the church, it seems likely that people simply left after receiving communion, and certainly that action would emphasize the need to go out into the world with Christ to serve him and make him known. By the end of the period of persecution, however, formal postcommunion prayers and a dismissal became common. Alternative postcommunion prayers are provided, the first a new composition and the second a modern revision of Cranmer's postcommunion prayer.

The Blessing

No blessing is needed, since the gift of communion is the greatest blessing we can receive. The Blessing seems to have been added first by bishops when they were present and then imitated by parish priests. Since Rite II makes the Blessing optional, it is possible to restore the original emphasis on moving out promptly into the world, but it is also possible to enrich the closing of the service with a variety of seasonal blessings.

Although a closing hymn also only delays our return to the world and our ministries and the Prayer Book says nothing about one, it remains a common custom and does allow the choir and clergy to exit in a formal way and to end, as we began, with a hymn of praise.

The Dismissal

A formal Dismissal corresponds to the formal salutation with which the service began. The brief, abrupt character of the Dismissal again stresses the urgency of being about God's work in the world. We are given communion not simply for our own sake, but for the sake of all God's people and God's world.

Four alternative Dismissals are provided, which can be varied to reflect seasonal themes. The first two, for example, might be used at Christmas to bear out the message of Christ's coming or the angels' message of peace, and the third sentence, speaking of the Spirit's power, is especially appropriate at Pentecost. The response to each is the same, enabling the congregation to respond without being delayed by having to look it up in the book.

In Easter Season, the joy of the resurrection is reflected by adding two Alleluias to the dismissal sentence and response.

Alternative Forms of the Great Thanksgiving (pages 367-375)
There is value in both continuity and variety. If the same prayer is used at every service, its familiarity may enable us to enter into it more deeply. The words can become a part of us, and we can pray them with the priest rather than wonder what will be said next. On the other hand, variety can re-enlist wandering attention and emphasize other aspects of our faith. No one eucharistic prayer can say everything that might be said. These alternative forms let us use other language on occasion yet still become familiar with each.

Eucharistic Prayer B
This prayer is similar in many ways to Prayer A but places somewhat more emphasis on the prophets, the incarnation, and the final coming of Christ. For these reasons it is often used at Christmas, Advent, and Epiphany. Some of the language is drawn from a second-century eucharistic prayer of Hippolytus; other phrases are by members of the commission who drafted this revision. References can be found to Ephesians 1:9-11, Colossians 1:15-20, 2 Thessalonians 2:13-14, and Hebrews 5:9 and 11:16.

Eucharistic Prayer C
Drafted by a member of the liturgical commission for the 1979 Prayer Book, this is the most "different" of the three alternatives. It provides for much more participation and obviously reflects a late twentieth-century understanding of the world as "our island home." The typically Anglican emphasis on creation is also in tune with modern environmental concerns. There are references to Genesis 26:7, Exodus 3:15-16, I Chronicles 12:17 and 29:18, Acts 3:13, 5:30, and 7:32, Hebrews 4:14, and 1 Peter 1:3.

Eucharistic Prayer D
This prayer, based on the Liturgy of St. Basil, is still widely used in the Orthodox Churches and was probably composed by Basil the Great in the late fourth century. In 1974 an ecumenical group of liturgical scholars from the Episcopal, Roman Catholic, and Protestant churches drafted this version of the prayer in hope that it

might provide a common eucharistic prayer. It has been authorized for use by the United Methodist Church and by a commission representing the major Lutheran Churches. In keeping with the tradition of the Latin church, it provides for the intercessions to be included here rather than in a separate prayer.

Notes About Customs

Chanting and Singing
Hymns, psalms, readings, and other parts of the service may be sung or chanted in some churches on some occasions.

Hymns are, in fact, a form of prayer. Usually they are written in a meter and set to music, because in that way the congregation can speak in unison most easily and because music adds beauty to the words.

Psalms are the ancient hymns of the Jewish people and are sung in a variety of ways. The oldest Christian music for the psalms is plainsong: chanting the psalms without harmony and, usually, without accompaniment. Anglican chant is a method of singing the psalms in harmony. Psalms can always be fitted to meter as "metrical psalms" and sung to hymn tunes.

Readings and various parts of the service are sometimes chanted, both because the music adds beauty and because the singing voice carries better and is more easily heard and understood in a large building.

Standing, Sitting, and Kneeling There was a time when a simple rule sufficed: stand to praise, sit to listen, kneel to pray. This rule has broken down in practice as we have learned more about ancient Christian customs, on the one hand, and have become more concerned for the disabled, on the other. We know now that the first Christians stood to pray because they saw themselves as set free from slavery. Standing to pray emphasizes our human dignity and value in God's sight. The Eastern churches have always stood for prayer, and this posture is becoming more common in Episcopal churches. It is also increasingly common to receive communion standing around the altar or coming in procession to "communion stations." Since it is also necessary for some people to stand for communion or to remain seated even for hymns and the Creed, no universal rules are available. Individual parishes may provide guidance in an order of worship to avoid confusion, but individuals should feel comfortable in acting on the basis of their own physical needs and spiritual preference so long as it is not disturbing to others.

Other Customs Some Christians cross themselves, bow, or genuflect (kneel briefly on one knee) at certain times in the service. These are ways of expressing our own devotion and are matters of individual preference. The sign of the cross is most often made at the end of the Creed and during the Absolution and Blessing. It is a way of acting out our acceptance of the statement being made. The Anglican and Benedictine custom has been to bow during the "incarnatus" in the Creed,when entering or leaving a pew, when passing an altar or the reserved sacrament, and when the cross is caried past in procession. Many Christians, however, genuflect at these points. Either custom is a way of expressing outwardly what we feel inwardly and should be a natural action for those who use it.

Glossary

Acolyte: Acolytes (or "servers") assist in the service by carrying a cross and torches, by helping to prepare the altar, and in other ways.

Alb: A full-length white vestment often worn by those assisting in a service.

Amice: A cloth collar often worn around the neck with an alb.

Advent: The four weeks before Christmas are known as Advent, which means "coming," and are used to prepare for Christ's coming, not only in

Bethlehem 2,000 years ago, but also in our lives today and at the end of time. The Gospel readings for Advent center on John the Baptist and the Virgin Mary, while the Old Testament readings deal with the prophecies of Christ's coming, especially in the prophet Isaiah. The traditional colors of the Advent season are blue, symbolizing heaven coming to earth and the Virgin Mary, and purple, the royal color of kings.

Bishop: The bishop, as the chief minister in each diocese and one called to serve as a successor to the apostles, symbolizes the unity of the church. The bishop is elected by the diocese and then ordained by at least three other bishops. The bishop alone can ordain priests and deacons, and the bishop alone can minister confirmation.

Cassock: Similar to an alb, a full-length vestment worn under other vestments; once used by clergy for every-day wear. The cassock is usually black, except in tropical countries and hot weather.

Ceremonial: The actions with which a liturgical service is performed. No eucharist could take place without ceremonial, since it is necessary to take, bless, break, and distribute bread and wine. The nature of the ceremonial reflects the importance of the service, the resources of the parish, the customs of the clergy and parishioners, and the importance the clergy and congregation place on what they are doing. Good ceremonial should help clarify the meaning of the service and involve people more deeply in it. It is helpful if the ceremonial has some consistency from age to age and from place to place so that we have a sense of continuity with the origins of the church and can move from one congregation to another with some sense of familiarity.

Chalice: The cup (usually of silver and often lined with gold) used for the wine at the eucharist.

Chasuble: A poncho-like vestment, often in the color of the season, which covers the other vestments, and may be worn by priests or bishops at the eucharist.

Cincture: A rope or belt worn around the waist with an alb or cassock.

Collect: A brief formal prayer designed to collect our thoughts around a particular theme. The accent is on the first syllable of the word.

Cope: A vestment like a cape, usually in the color of the season, which is most often worn by bishops but may be worn by other clergy and lay people as well, especially in processions.

Cranmer, Thomas: Thomas Cranmer was Archbishop of Canterbury from 1532 to 1556 and was the chief author of the first English Prayer Book. His sensitivity to the beauty and power of language created the tradition of Prayer Book language that still shapes Anglican worship.

Deacon: A deacon is an ordained person whose calling is to represent Christ and the church, especially to those in need, and who is authorized to read the Gospel and assist in the ministration of the sacraments. A deacon cannot preside at a celebration of the eucharist or give blessings or absolutions.

Decalogue: Literally "Ten Words," a title for the Ten Commandments.

Epiphany: The season following Christmas, centering on the baptism of Christ and the revelation of Christ as a light to the nations of the world.

Eucharist: One of the titles used for the central Christian act of worship, this title comes from the Greek word for "thanksgiving." As Jesus gave thanks to God over the bread and wine at the Last Supper, so we give thanks for the life, death, and resurrection of Jesus when we gather in his presence.

Lay Eucharistic Minister: A lay person licensed to assist with the ministration of communion and, if authorized, to carry the sacrament to those who are shut in.

Lay Reader: Someone not ordained but licensed by the bishop to assist in the conduct of services on a regular basis. Lay Readers may, where there is need, conduct non-sacramental services and may also be licensed to preach.

Lectionary: The readings and psalms appointed for particular days. Today most of the liturgical churches read selections from the Bible in a three-year cycle in which the Gospel according to St. Matthew is the primary source for "Year A," the Gospel according to St. Mark is the primary source for readings in "Year B," and the Gospel according to St. Luke is the primary source for "Year C." The other New Testament books are read in a similar pattern: Acts and Revelation in Easter Season, 1 Corinthians in Epiphany, Romans in Pentecost of Year A, and so on. The Old Testament readings are usually chosen for their relationship with the Gospel readings, though it is customary to read the prophets, especially Isaiah, in Advent. The Episcopal version of the lectionary is found on pages 889-931 of the Prayer Book. There is also a Daily Office Lectionary with readings and psalms in a two-year cycle on pages 936 to 1001.

Lent: The forty days (not including Sundays) before Easter have been set aside since the early Middle Ages as a time of special prayer and penitence in preparation for Easter. The English custom was to keep the season by using stark simplicity in vestments made of sackcloth or unbleached linen. The Roman custom, widely used in other churches also, is to use vestments of purple.

Liturgy: Deriving from a Greek word meaning "public activity," this word has come to refer to the public corporate activity of Christians, more especially to worship, and in particular the eucharist.

Liturgical Churches: A term used to indicate that a church has a set form of worship, usually centered on the eucharist, rather than a free form of worship centered on the sermon. The Anglican, Orthodox, and Roman Catholic Churches are liturgical churches, while the so-called evangelical churches tend to be non-liturgical. In recent years there has been a trend toward more liturgical worship in the major Protestant churches.

Mass: A traditional title for the Eucharist which goes back to at least the sixth century. It seems to be drawn from the dismissal at the end of the service, *Ite missa es*.

Minister: A general term used for all who serve God. Every Christian has a ministry, but some Christians have their primary ministry in the formal life and worship of the church, while most have their primary ministry in the world. The Prayer Book says there are four orders of ministry: bishops, priests, deacons, and lay people. The first three are sometimes called the "ordained ministry."

Miter: The pointed, divided hat often worn by a bishop. It represents the tongues of fire that rested on the apostles at Pentecost.

37

Paten: The plate, usually of silver, used for the eucharistic bread.

Pentecost: The celebration of the gift of the Holy Spirit (see Acts 2:1-12). This gift was given at the time of a Jewish festival called Pentecost because it took place fifty days after Passover. The Christian celebration takes place fifty days after Easter. The usual color of the day is red, symbolizing the flames of fire in which the Spirit came upon the apostles.

Preface: The introduction to the Prayer of Consecration. It follows the Sursum corda and ends in the Sanctus. A Proper Preface is also provided for certain seasons and holy days.

Priest: The priest is ordained to a ministry of Word and Sacrament and normally serves as the chief minister in each parish. Priests also serve in teaching and healing ministries and sometimes combine secular vocations with the work of priesthood.

Propers: The Collect and Readings for a particular day or season.

Rector: A priest who has been elected to serve as chief ordained minister in an Episcopal parish. Rectors usually preside at vestry meetings and have tenure.

Ritual: Technically, ritual is the form of words used in a service. It is often improperly used to refer to the ceremonial with which the words are acted out.

Sarum Rite: The liturgical customs of Salisbury (Sarum) Cathedral were very influential in pre-Reformation England and continue to have an influence on Anglican liturgy. Such customs as the use of sackcloth for Lenten vestments and blue for Advent are especially common in Episcopal churches.

Stole: A long band of cloth worn around the neck by a priest and over one shoulder by a deacon. It is usually in the color of the season and may have various symbols on it.

Surplice: A loose-fitting white vestment worn over a cassock by priests, acolytes, and choir members.

Vicar: Usually, a priest who is appointed by the bishop to serve in a smaller church or mission.

Suggestions for Further Reading

Hatchett, Marion, *Commentary on the American Prayer Book*, New York, Seabury Press, 1980. This is the standard reference work for the 1979 Book of Common Prayer and the place where answers to most questions about it will be found.

Other books that might be helpful to a deeper understanding of liturgical worship and the Anglican tradition include the following. Many of these are out of print and not likely to be in your local library, but a good parish library shoiuld have them and a parish priest may be willing to lend them to those who care enough to ask.

Bouyer, Louis, *Liturgical Piety*, Notre Dame, Indiana, University of Notre Dame Press, 1954. Written by a French Roman Catholic and out of date because it was written before Vatican II but still an excellent discussion of the origins and development of Christian worship.

Casel, Odo, *The Mystery of Christian Worship*, Westminster, Md., The Newman Press, 1962. Casel was a very influential Roman Catholic monk whose writing helps relate Christian worship to the broader background of the first century world and show how the basic pattern of Christian worship developed.

Dix, Dom Gregory, *The Shape of the Liturgy*, London, Dacre Press, 1945. A classic history of the development of the liturgy from its Jewish origins to the twentieth century; beautifully written, but also somewhat dated and more detailed than many people will want.

Price, Charles, and Louis Weil, *Liturgy for Living*, New York, Seabury Press, 1979. One chapter on the meaning of worship, one on the history of the Prayer Book, and then several chapters about the various sections of the Prayer Book; this was written for the ordinary church member and provides a good introduction.

Otto, Rudolf, *The Idea of the Holy*, New York, Oxford University Press, 1950. This is one of the great books on the thoughts and feelings that underlie the human response to God.

Shepherd, Massey, *At All Times and in All Places*, Greenwich, Conn.., Seabury Press, 1953. Six nicely done stories about the celebration of the eucharist in six ages of church history. The final chapter glimpses the future in 1960!

Shepherd, Massey, *The Oxford American Prayer Book Commentary*, New York, Oxford University Press, 1950. This commentary is based on the 1928 Prayer Book and provides a facing page of commentary for every page of text for the whole book except the Psalter. While obviously out of date, it is still a helpful source of information and easy to use because of its format.

Stuhlman, Byron, *Eucharistic Celebration*, 1789-1979, New York, Church Hymnal Corporation, 1991. A discussion of the development of the American Prayer Book from its English origins to the present time.

Underhill, Evelyn, *Worship*, New York, Harper and Brothers, 1936. A well-written history of the development of patterns of worship from primitive societies to the twentieth century; written by an English woman sixty years ago but still a good place to begin.

Wright, J. Robert, *Prayer Book Spirituality*, New York, Church Hymnal Corporation, 1991. Selections from three centuries of devotional commentary on the Book of Common Prayer.

Index

41